# Magic and Magicians

by Michael Burgess

**Published By**
**Capstone Press, Inc.**
**Mankato, Minnesota USA**

**Distributed By**
 CHILDRENS PRESS®
CHICAGO

# CIP
## LIBRARY OF CONGRESS CATALOGING IN PUBLICATION DATA

Burgess, Michael.
    Magic and magicians / by Michael Burgess.
        p. cm. – (The Unexplained)
    Summary: Discusses past and present manifestations of magic, both the
    supernatural kind and the magic illusions created as a form of entertainment.

    ISBN 1-56065-044-3:
    1. Magic – Juvenile literature. 2. Conjuring – Juvenile literature.
    3. Magicians – History – Juvenile literature. [1. Magic. 2. Magic tricks.
    3. Magicians.] I. Title. II. Series.
    BF1601.B87    1990
    133.4'3–dc 20 – dc20                                89-39672
                                                           CIP
                                                           AC

## PHOTO CREDITS

Excalibur Hotel & Casino, Las Vegas: 4
Irving Desfor: 12, 19, 32, 40, 45
Michael Jacobs: 6, 20, 27, 28, 48
The Childrens Theatre: 16

## CAPSTONE PRESS
Box 669, Mankato, MN 56001

# Contents

# Introduction

Imagine that you live in a deep forest. You have lived in the forest all of your life. You have never left the forest, not even once. You have never heard of radio or television. You have seen lightning, but you have never seen a light bulb.

It would be a very different world, wouldn't it?

Now, imagine one day a stranger enters the forest. The stranger is friendly. You invite her to share your fire. Suddenly, there is a sound. A twig snaps, leaves rustle. Frightened, you peer into the shadows. The stranger pulls a shiny metal tube from her pocket. She presses a button. Click, there is a beam of light.

Would you believe this stranger had **supernatural** powers? That she was a magician? A sorceress? A medicine woman?

You might, if you had never seen a flashlight.

In the world of **magic**, things are seldom what they seem. Have you ever been to a magic show? Seen a magician pull a rabbit from a hat? Seen ladies floating above the stage? Or seen them disappear in a puff of smoke, or be sawed in two before your very eyes?

This is the world of magic.

It is a world filled with **wizards**, **fairies**, **sorcerers**, **witches**, and **elves**. A world with swords in stones, ropes that hang in the air, secret words, and wands that work wonders. Magic is a world of genies and black cats, evil curses, and people who escape from locked trunks.

Are you ready for the world of magic?

Then watch closely—for things are not always what they seem.

# What is Magic?

Before we explore the wonders of magic, we must first decide what magic is.

Those familiar with this world would have us divide magic into two parts: True Magic and **Illusion**. Often, they are not easy to tell apart.

Legends tell of King Arthur's teacher, Merlin, a wizard. If wizards were real, they would be considered True Magicians. The Great Houdini (1874-1926) was a famous **escape artist.** We regard him as an Illusionist.

Both created powerful magic.

## True Magic

The dictionary defines magic as "having power over nature." What exactly does this mean? In many ways, we all have power over nature. The difference is, the magician's power is said to be supernatural—or, beyond nature.

True magic is a way of looking at the world. It is a way of seeing and believing. The word "magic" also means "the **science** of the **Magi**".

Long ago, Magi were wise men and teachers. In their world, all of nature was alive. Not only animals and trees, but stones and stars and things we cannot see. All were parts of a great whole. All of the parts were connected.

Much like scientists studying the secrets of the universe today, the Magi believed there was more to the world than meets the eye. They believed that by learning how the forces of nature work, they could learn to make things happen that would not happen otherwise.

## True Magic and Alchemy

Have you ever heard of the alchemists (Al-kem-ists?) Alchemists lived long ago and were said to be able to turn lead into gold.

Were they really able to do it? Some say yes, but scientists say no. We do know that Isaac Newton, the man who first explained gravity, was an alchemist. **Alchemy** eventually grew into a science called chemistry.

It is also said that true magicians can see events and overhear conversations happening in faraway places. Not long ago, being in two places at once by riding on invisible waves would indeed have been magic. Today, we put these magic powers in boxes and call them telephones, radio, and television.

The music we hear and the news that we see come to us simultaneously (at the same time) from stations far away. They are even beamed to us from satellites in space. They are carried by invisible waves of electricity.

Not magical enough for you ?

Well, did you know that no one has ever seen a particle of electricity—an electron? All that we know is what electrons do.

Think about this for a moment. When you switch on your reading lamp, you are controlling invisible forces able to turn darkness into light.

Is science "true magic?" Is true magic "science?"

# Illusion

Illusionists are also people of power. They have the power to make us believe we have seen something we have not.

Perhaps the greatest illusionist of all time was Harry Houdini. He was called the Great Houdini for a good reason. His feats were truly amazing. There were no handcuffs that could hold the Great Houdini. No ropes or chains could bind him. No locked chest was secure enough to contain him. No matter what you put the Great Houdini into, he escaped from it. Even underwater.

Magic? Supernatural powers? Only if you do not know how to do what Houdini did.

Harry Houdini was an "escape artist." Houdini's magic was his strength, his agility, and his talent for picking locks. He told people that he had no supernatural powers. Many never believed him.

There are other illusionists with amazing tricks. (We call them "tricks" because they trick us.) Have you seen a **fakir** (fah-KEER) of India charm a cobra, a very deadly snake, with a flute? The cobra is "charmed" by the motion of the fakir, who weaves back and forth as he plays. Does the snake even hear the music? Not as you and I would. The magic is in believing that the cobra is charmed.

The greatest fakir trick of all is the famous Hindu Rope trick. In this feat of illusion, the fakir places a coiled rope in a large clay urn, or pot. He then sits down and charms the rope with his flute. As the audience watches, the rope slowly rises from the urn.

Magic?

No. It is very good illusion. In this trick, the fakir's "rope" is actually made of sections of bamboo or hollowed bone. From a secret compartment under the urn, the fakir's hidden helper threads a thin pole into the "rope." As the fakir plays, the rope rises up into the air.

At least that is what the audience sees. As we said, in the world of magic, you must believe what you see.

# Magic Through The Ages

There has been magic of one sort or another for as long as there have been people. In the hills of southern France, for example, there are several large caves. People lived in these caves for hundreds, perhaps thousands, of years. On the walls, they painted pictures of deer, birds, bison, and wooly mammoths. Alongside the animals are stick figures of men carrying spears.

The paintings are pictures of hunts. We now believe that the pictures were magic "spells" put on the walls to make sure the hunt was successful. The pictures were **charms**. They were like wishing on a star or petting a rabbit's foot.

Magic was a strong belief in ancient Egypt. The Egyptian "Magi" were said to be very powerful. They possessed a secret knowledge. They were certainly great astronomers and mathematicians. How the Great Pyramids were built is still a mystery. The blocks of stone used to build them each weigh thousands of pounds. There are millions of these blocks. Historians and engineers shake their heads and say that even with thousands of slaves and many, many years, the pyramids could not have been built. Did the ancient Egyptians know more than we think?

Do you know the story of Moses? This wise man led the people of Israel out of slavery in Egypt. To the Jews (and later to the Christians) Moses was a prophet. To the Egyptians, Moses was a great magician. What would you call someone who raised a stick and parted the Red Sea?

Aaron was another slave of the pharaoh (FAIR-oh), an Egyptian king. In front of the pharaoh, Aaron turned his staff (or wand) into a snake. When the pharaoh's magicians tried the same trick, Aaron's snake ate their snakes. According to the story, the pharaoh was very impressed.

Ancient Egypt was a land that breathed mystery and magic. The same was true of ancient Greece.

Consider the many oracles (OR-uh-kuls) of this ancient land. An oracle was a person who went into a trance and predicted the future. As you might guess, oracles were important people if their predictions came true. When they did not, the oracles were often put to death.

Greek myths are filled with magic. There are tales of winged horses, enchanted pools, and magic flutes. The ancient Greeks believed the gods of nature were all around them. If you knew how to ask, they would help you accomplish great deeds. Not all of the magic was good. One sorceress, Medusa (Meh-DOO-sah) turned men into stone. Another turned them into pigs. One poor woman wound up as a spider.

According to our ancestors, all of nature was alive. Trees and sky, streams and mountains, meadows and dark glades had their own spirits. There were fire spirits, water spirits, spirits of the air, and spirits of the earth.

Do you recognize these spirits? They are the elves and **leprechauns** (LEP-reh-kahns), fairy princesses and gnomes (nomes). In the world of magic, fairy tales come true.

You probably remember King Arthur and his Knights of the Round Table. According to one story, Merlin, the magician of King Arthurs' court, made Excalibur (ExCALibur). This was King Arthur's magical sword. The legend tells that young Arthur proved he was the true king by pulling Excalibur from a stone. Many had tried and only Arthur succeeded.

Another story tells how King Arthur sent his knights to search for the **Holy Grail.** It was said to be the source of all things. A magical fountain in a golden cup. King Arthur's kingdom of Camelot was in ruins. Only the magic of the Grail could save it. Only the purest knight was said to be capable of bringing it back. This is a moral common to tales of true magic. Magical power is said to be granted, or earned, only by the pure of heart.

# The Philosopher's Stone

The alchemist had one important goal. It was to find the **Philosopher's Stone**. With it, magicians believed that any substance could be turned into pure gold.

Around A.D. 1400, an alchemist named Helvetius (Hel-VEE-shus) claimed to have found the stone. It was described as clear and shiny, like glass. Helvetius said it was given to him by a mysterious stranger. According to the story, doubters gathered as Helvetius put a tiny piece of the stone into a container of metal. Moments later, the metal was transformed into gold. The gold was taken to a metalsmith. The metalsmith confirmed it was pure.

Was this true magic, or only illusion? Did Helvetius really have the Philosopher's Stone? We will never know for certain. As the story ends Helvetius seems forever after to have had plenty of gold.

Alchemists and wizards were common in Europe during what we call the Dark Ages. Many of our beliefs about magicians come from this time. Magicians knew the powers of crystals. (Today, we use crystals to create laser beams.) Magicians knew the "healing arts." (Today, we call these wizards "doctors.")

# Witches

Witches were female magicians believed to possess secret powers. They cast spells, made potions and, it was said, rode broomsticks. Many of them were nurses and midwives. They knew the secrets of herbs and how to deliver babies.

If your child was ill and a woman cured it with a potion, you might consider this magic. Even today, we use vaccines and antibiotics that are "miracles" of modern medicine. Unfortunately, witches were also blamed when someone got sick. Too often, deaths seemed mysterious and went unexplained. A fatal heart attack might seem a cruel death "caused by a witch's evil eye." Whenever cows stopped giving milk, or chickens stopped laying eggs, witches were often blamed.

Thousands of witches were put to death by hanging, drowning, or being burned at the stake. In the year 1620, in Salem, Massachusetts, 20 witches were burned at the stake. All over Europe, witches were hunted down. In a single day in 1641, in the city of Malmo in Sweden, 23 adults and 15 children were put to death for practicing "the black arts." All were considered witches.

People's fears made them cruel. They devised a "test" to find "real" witches. The test was called "swimming." The woman's left hand was tied to her right foot. Her right hand was tied to her left foot. Then she was thrown into the river. Witches, as everyone "knew," floated. So, if the woman was lucky enough to keep her head above water and not drown, she was put to death. If she sank, she was innocent.

# Famous Men Of Magic

Simon Magus (MAH-gus) lived in the time of Jesus. He was said to be a powerful magician. People claimed he could fly, cast spells, walk through fire, and make himself invisible. When the Roman emperor Nero ordered Simon Magus' head cut off, the magician enchanted Nero's guards. The guards set him free. When Simon Magus walked into Nero's royal chamber, the emperor was so impressed he made him his court magician.

## Paracelsus

Paracelsus' (PAIR-uh-SEL-sus) real name was Theophrastus Bombastus von Hohenheim. He was a very accomplished doctor. He is said to have cured a paralyzed young girl with only a glass of salt water.

Paracelsus was also an early hypnotist. Doctors now know that hypnotism can help a person recover from an illness. If you believe you will get well, you are more likely to. Today, we call this "the power of positive thinking," "imaging," and "biofeedback." People in the Dark Ages called it magic.

## Nicholas Flamel

Nicholas Flamel (Flah-MEL) lived in Paris between 1330 and 1418. Until he was 52, Flamel was a poor man. He was a scribe, barely able to feed his family on the pennies he made lettering manuscripts. These were the days before the printing press. If you wanted a book, someone had to copy it for you by hand.

In 1382, a strange volume fell into Nicholas Flamel's hands. It was a very old book. It was large and decorated with gold. The pages were not, according to Flamel, made of paper or parchment. Instead, they seemed to be made from the bark of trees.

Flamel's hobby was alchemy. The book supposedly held the secret of turning lead into gold. Did Nicholas Flamel actually do it? No one knows. We do know that, suddenly, Flamel and his wife were very rich. They gave large sums of gold to hospitals and churches and supported many widows and orphans.

Where did the gold come from? Nicholas Flamel claimed he made it. He even said, once you knew how, it was really very easy.

## Giuseppi Desa

Giuseppi Desa (Joo-SEH-pee DAY-say) was a monk who lived in Italy around 1600. Widely known for his kindness, he is known to the church as St. Joseph of Copertino—the Flying Monk.

They called him this because, on several occasions in front of many witnesses, Giuseppi Desa was seen to fly from the floor of the chapel to the top of the altar.

## Crazy Horse

Crazy Horse was a great chief of the tribe of Native Americans called the Sioux (Soo). The Sioux lived on the Great Plains. As a boy, Crazy Horse had a dream called a **vision**. Native Americans believe that visions show us some secrets of nature.

In his vision, Crazy Horse rode a magical horse. Both he and the horse were invisible. They could not be harmed. Whenever Crazy Horse rode into battle, he went into his vision world and rode his magical steed.

Did Crazy Horse really become invisible? Was he a true magician? Who can say? We do know that many times Crazy Horse galloped back and forth in front of his enemies and was never wounded in battle.

## Aleister Crowley

Aleister Crowley was an Englishman who lived and practiced magic in the first half of this century. Crowley was a mystic (one who studies mysteries), a mountain climber, and a poet. Crowley and his bride spent their wedding night in the Great Pyramid in Egypt. They both claimed that, after they performed a magical ceremony, the dark room was filled with a blue light. The light was so bright they were able to read without candles.

Aleister Crowley was a serious student and scholar. He formed his own magical group. He once walked across the Sahara Desert calling up spirits. Supposedly, these spirits answered. Crowley said they shared many secrets with him. Eye witnesses claimed the magician could make himself invisible.

One former doubter told a story about walking with Crowley down a street in New York City. Crowley picked out a stranger and began walking close behind him. As they walked, the magician imitated the stranger's posture and stride. Then, suddenly, Aleister Crowley dropped to his knees on the pavement. A few paces ahead, the stranger did the same.

### Leonid Vasiliev

In the 1920s, a Russian named Leonid Vasiliev(LAY-oh-nid- Vah-SIL-ie-ef) convinced others he was able to put people to sleep. Simple hypnotism? Not quite. Vasiliev seemed able to do this at a distance. The person being hypnotized was not even aware of the experiment. In one instance, Vasiliev reportedly put someone to sleep in another city that was a thousand miles away.

# Peter Hurkos (1911-1988)

Peter Hurkos may not have been a magician, but many believe he possessed strange mental powers. As a young man, Hurkos fell from a ladder and fractured his skull. When he awoke in the hospital, he discovered that he could read the minds of those around him. He was also able to form pictures of people from objects linked to them. Police departments from all over the world asked Peter Hurkos to help them solve mysterious crimes. Many times, as in the famous Boston Strangler case of the 1970s, he gave descriptions and clues that led to the capture of a criminal. Hurkos had no explanation for his powers. Neither do we.

## Dr. Rolf Alexander

Rolf Alexander is a New Zealand doctor with an unusual ability. Dr. Alexander claims he can make clouds go away by staring at them. In September, 1954, a camera crew from a Canadian television network recorded just such a feat on film. Dr. Alexander stood, at 2:00 p.m., staring at a large cloud. By 2:14, the cloud was nearly gone. Three minutes later, it had disappeared completely.

## Uri Geller

No list of magicians would be complete without Uri Geller. According to stories about him, Uri wandered into a neighbor's garden as a boy. Suddenly, he saw a large, transparent bowl in the sky. A figure reportedly came out of the bowl. He flashed a beam of light into Uri's eyes. Uri immediately fell asleep. When he awoke, Geller says he was possessed of new and strange powers. Uri Geller is most famous for his "trick" of bending spoons. He strokes them with his finger. He is also able to move the hands on watches. In one recorded instance, he actually raised the mercury in a thermometer eight degrees just by looking at it. Although no one has discovered Geller's secrets, experts suspect he is more an entertainer than a wizard.

## Harry Blackstone

Harry Blackstone is a modern illusionist. His father, the Great Blackstone, was called "America's Wizard." When the younger Blackstone was in college, he passed his final exams by elevating a man, a piano, a horse, and a 12-piece orchestra on the auditorium stage. He has also made an elephant disappear. His most famous trick is called The Floating Lightbulb. The bulb not only floats in midair, it shines without a source of electricity. No one, not even other magicians, know how Harry Blackstone does it.

## Siegfried and Roy

Siegfried and Roy are modern illusionists whose specialty is making animals appear and disappear, as if by magic. White tigers, panthers, leopards, lions, horses, pythons, elephants, and even a duck. The climax of Siegfried and Roy's performance comes when they are "eaten" by a huge mechanical dragon—only to reappear seconds later, swinging from ropes over the stage.

## David Copperfield

David Copperfield is the master of modern illusionists. Some people say he has strange powers. He is able to ignite matches, explode light bulbs, and bend crowbars without touching them. His most famous "trick" involved a safe. He was locked inside of it. The safe was put on the 20th floor of a building. Then the building was blown up. A camera showed Copperfield's hand coming out of the safe 20 seconds before the explosion. Immediately after, he emerged from under a tarp a quarter of a mile away. Magic or Illusion? Only David Copperfield knows the answer.

# Magic? Or Illusion?

We have divided magic into two parts—true magic and illusion.

Those who practice true magic say you must know how nature works to be a true magician. The true magician spends his life learning. True magicians believe in supernatural powers. They also believe that magic is the world in front of us.

Illusion is pretend magic. The word illusion means "to deceive or be deceived." Illusionists are tricksters of the highest sort. Their tricks depend on our willingness to be fooled. Illusionists know that we want to see the impossible and believe the unbelievable.

Why? Because it is fun. Why is it fun? Because it makes us see the world in new ways.

Illusionists have been around for a long time. We have read about the fakirs of India. For at least a thousand years, fakirs have performed their magic. In the market place today, they still swallow swords, eat fire, and charm ropes.

Illusionists are entertainers. Singers sing, dancers dance, and illusionists amaze.

In Europe during the Middle Ages, true magic was thought to be fading. Illusionists, however, joined entertainers who traveled from market to market and fair to fair.

Every king and queen had a court magician. Every castle became a stage for illusionists. Through the power of illusion, magicians turned stone rooms into magical kingdoms. Coins disappeared, handkerchiefs changed color, and balls vanished into thin air.

A clever young person could learn a few tricks, go out on the road, and seek his or her fortune. Over the years, some very remarkable tricks were mastered. Illusionists traded tricks and improved and expanded their magic.

Around the year 1800, some very famous illusionists began to appear in Europe. The first of these was Alex Herrmann. Herrmann was a serious student of magic. He traveled as far as India and Tibet to learn the tricks of the fakirs. Soon he was performing before kings and queens and filling concert halls.

He passed his tricks on to his younger brother Carl. Carl became known throughout Europe as Herrmann the Great. From what we know, he was a master illusionist.

Herrmann the Great could pluck coins from empty air and lighted cigars from beards—all right before the eyes of his audience. When the lights went down, Herrmann the Great could make a woman float in mid-air! (Actually, she was resting on a draped platform. The audience saw what they wanted to see.) Even eating dinner with Herrmann the Great was a magical experience. Gold coins somehow appeared inside biscuits. Wine glasses disappeared without a trace.

Magic? No, but a very good illusion.

# The Great Houdini

By far, the most famous of all illusionists was a man named Harry Houdini. Houdini's real name was Erich Weiss. He was born in Appleton, Wisconsin, in 1874.

As a boy, he was fascinated with card and coin tricks. He practiced his tricks with a friend at the necktie factory where they worked. By the time he was 17, young Erich was a professional magician.

He took his stage name from another famous illusionist, Robert Houdin. Houdin practiced his magic in Paris before Herrmann the Great. He was a great illusionist indeed. In addition to the usual tricks of floating ladies, disappearing coins, and magical trunks, Houdin was able to "see" objects while blindfolded. Members of the audience would hold up objects while Houdin talked to his assistant about this and that. The magician was able to identify the objects every time.

Magic? No. The trick involved an elaborate code used by Houdin and his assistant.

But some of Robert Houdin's tricks were truly amazing. Newspapers of the time reported orange trees sprouting and blossoming on stage. Houdin actually threw the blossoms to the audience. Houdin often closed his performance by walking among the audience with a bottle. He was able to pour whatever drink he was asked for from the bottle. The water was pure, the juice was sweet, and the wine flavorful. To this day, no one knows how Houdin did this trick.

The Great Houdini did not become instantly famous. For more than a year, he performed with his brother Jacob in beer halls and saloons in New York City. One of Houdini's first illusions was one he had learned from Robert Houdin: the Trunk Substitution Trick.

Someone from the audience, usually a sailor, would come on stage. They would bind Houdini securely with heavy ropes. He was then put into a large canvas bag. The bag was then tied with more rope. It was sealed with candle wax and placed in a large trunk. Finally, the trunk was covered with heavy straps and, just to make sure, padlocked.

Surely, no one could escape from this.

Houdini's brother Jacob then placed the trunk in a large, empty cabinet and pulled the curtain. Jacob told the audience to watch closely. Then he stepped behind the curtain. At the very same moment, Houdini jumped out.

True magic? No, but illusion at its very best. Here is how the Trunk Substitution trick worked.

For years, Houdini had practiced untying knots. His

hands were extremely strong. His body was very athletic and limber. Having his hands tied behind his back presented no problem. By the time Houdini was placed in the canvas bag, his hands were already free.

As soon as the bag was sealed and put into the trunk, Houdini slit the bottom of the bag with a sharp blade. The audience thought they were seeing a bound man in a sealed bag put inside a padlocked trunk covered with heavy straps. What was really there was young Harry Houdini waiting to pop out.

But wait—what about the trunk? How was Houdini able to escape from that? A secret panel, of course.

From inside the trunk, Houdini opened the escape door and crawled out. By the time Jacob was telling the audience to watch closely, Houdini was already standing just behind the curtain. As his brother stepped through, Houdini jumped out.

The audience, of course, was quite amazed. But there was more to come.

When the applause died down, Houdini opened the curtain. Where had his brother Jacob gone? The trunk was opened. The bag was lifted out, untied and unsealed. There was Jacob, sitting (so he could hide the slit in the bag's bottom) with his hands securely bound behind him. How had he managed this? By merely reversing Houdini's escape.

Word of Houdini's magic powers spread. The young magician worked hard at his craft. He practiced long hours. He learned all he could from other illusionists. He also invented new tricks of his own.

One of his most famous was the Needle Trick. As the audience watched, Houdini put 12 sewing needles into his mouth, one by one. He followed the needles with a piece of thread. Then, the magic began. With all eyes on him, Houdini twisted his mouth this way and that. Finally, he pulled 12 threaded needles from his mouth.

Can you guess how he did it? The threaded needles were already hidden in Houdini's mouth. The unthreaded ones stayed there until he went backstage.

Does such trickery make Houdini a fake and a cheat? Not at all. They make him an illusionist. He is an artist who practices make believe. He helps us fool ourselves.

Does this mean The Great Houdini was not, like true magicians, a man of power? Once again, no. Houdini's magic lay in his own abilities. He was a strong athlete and a good swimmer. By training very hard, he was able to perform feats others simply could not.

Soon, there was no padlock or set of handcuffs Houdini could not master. Magic? No, he was just the world's best locksmith. He was "The Great Houdini! Handcuff King and Escape Artist!" He made $12 a week, a lot of money for a young man at that time.

Year by year, Houdini's talents and fame grew. He publicly challenged anyone to construct a pair of handcuffs from which he could not escape. Police departments and locksmiths from all over the world tried their best. No matter what sort of handcuffs they came up with, Houdini handed them back, opened. Once, he even escaped from the famous Scotland Yard in London. He had been handcuffed and placed naked in a cell. Police had not detected the small tool Houdini used to pick the locks.

Nothing could hold the Great Houdini. Not even a strait jacket. A strait jacket is a special coatlike device used to prevent people from hurting themselves or others. The long sleeves of the strait jacket are crossed over the chest. They are then strapped securely behind the back. Until Houdini came along, no one had ever escaped from one.

Houdini accomplished it, not with magic, but by being a **contortionist** (kun-TOR-shun-ist). A contortionist is able to twist his or her body into unnatural positions. Houdini was limber enough to pull one arm from the strait jacket's sleeves. He then freed the other. By twisting the jacket around, he was able to unbuckle the straps with his teeth. For added surprise, Houdini always rebuckled the straps before giving the strait jacket back.

The Great Houdini was most famous for his underwater escapes. To this day, no one has been able to match them.

For years, Houdini practiced holding his breath. Eventually, by the magic of hard work, he was able to stay completely submerged for five or six minutes. To make it even harder, he practiced untying himself underwater in bathtubs filled with blocks of ice.

At last, the day came when the Great Houdini was ready to amaze the world. It was on a cold day in late November of 1907. Houdini, wearing handcuffs, leaped from a bridge into the Detroit River. A minute passed. Then two, then three. Just when the crowd began to worry, Houdini bobbed to the surface. He waved the handcuffs.

Those who could not believe their eyes had the chance to see it again. In the spring, 40,000 people watched Houdini repeat the escape. In the summer, Houdini jumped from a San Francisco bridge. Handcuffed, of course. A 75 lb. metal ball was chained to his feet. This time, while Houdini worked to free himself, he was being dragged to the bottom. Fortunately, it only took the magician two minutes to work loose.

For the next 20 years, the Great Houdini toured the world, one of the most amazing men of his time. Wherever he went, crowds gathered. They came to watch this small, muscular man accomplish the impossible. Houdini was lowered into frozen rivers through holes cut in the ice. He was handcuffed and submerged in metal boxes secured with large bolts. He was chained and placed in milk containers filled with water.

No matter how often he did these things, people could not believe their eyes. Houdini told them over and over that there was nothing magic or supernatural about his feats. Many fans refused to believe him. They had seen him do the impossible.

In the Water Torture cell, Houdini was lowered head first into a tank filled with water. His ankles were firmly locked in wooden blocks. The front of the torture cell was glass. As the curtains were drawn, the audience watched Houdini struggling to get free. This trick was perhaps his best.

Before a performance in the fall of 1926, Houdini was injured. He enjoyed testing his stomach muscles by inviting people to punch him as hard as they could. One challenger caught Houdini off guard and his muscles were relaxed. This time, the magic did not work. Houdini knew at once he was badly hurt.

Although he was in great pain, Houdini went through with his performance. He barely escaped from the ankle blocks in the water torture cell. The pain grew worse during the night. Houdini was taken to the hospital. The blow to his stomach had broken the illusionist's appendix. The next morning on Halloween, the Great Houdini died.

# Do You Believe In Magic?

When we began our trip into the world of magic, we asked ourselves what magic was. Have we found out? Look back at what we have seen.

Much of what we thought was magic turned out to be illusion. Tricks are performed by clever people to entertain us. A good magic trick turns the world upside down. It makes the impossible happen and shakes our belief in the way things are. In the world of illusion, seeing is believing.

True magic is said to be a different thing. You might say it is what illusion pretends to be. Is there true magic? Science says no.

Some people say the age of magic is over. Science has taken us beyond fairy tales and superstition. Has it really? Is magic gone? Or have we just learned to accomplish magic with machines instead of wands? Perhaps magic is only hiding.

Compare magic and science for a moment. The alchemists believed that the world was made of four elements: fire, air, water, and earth. Science now tells us that the world is made of atoms. The atoms are made of particles.

There are four of them: the proton, electron, neutron, and photon. We have never seen any of these particles. How different are they from fairies and elves?

At one time, people believed that the world was filled with unseen spirits. Now we know it is filled with unseen forces. Are spirits forces? Are magic and science saying the same thing?

Do magical curses work? Can someone put a "hex" on us? Before you laugh and say no, ask yourself these questions. Has anyone ever said something to you so mean it ruined your whole day? Something so nice it made the whole world seem brighter? Are these magic "spells?"

What about charms? Have you ever had a lucky cap? Perhaps a baseball mitt that never dropped the ball? A special stone you carried in your pocket and rubbed when you made a wish? If we do not believe in magic, why are there charm bracelets? Why do we look for a four-leaf clover? Or knock on wood?

If flying on a carpet is magic, what about flying in an airplane? If leprechauns and elves are magic, what are electrons and gravity? If we cannot be in two places at once, how do we explain using a telephone?

Is there true magic? Before you decide, listen to the story of Tecumseh.

Tecumseh (Teh-KUM-seh) was a Native American, a great chief of the Shawnee tribe. He lived in Ohio during the time of the Revolutionary War. Tecumseh's dream was to unite all of the tribes east of the Mississippi River. His dream was so strong that, for many months, he traveled the country alone. He talked to other chiefs and persuaded them to join him. Most of the chief's agreed. They believed in Tecumseh's vision. One chief, however, did not.

Tecumseh did not argue with this chief. It would have been disrespectful. Tecumseh only handed the chief a handful of black sticks. He told the chief to burn one of the sticks in the fire each full moon. He said that when the last stick was gone, the ground would shake. The trees would fall and the rivers move. Tecumseh also told the chief his village would be destroyed. The year was 1812.

Each full moon, the chief burned one of Tecumseh's sticks. Finally, the last stick was gone. Days later, a great earthquake struck the Mississippi Valley. Scientists believe it was the largest earthquake ever to strike the United States. It was larger even than the great San Francisco earthquake of 1906. Witnesses reported that the Great Plains rolled like waves on the ocean. The Mississippi River changed its course. With a sound like thunder in the earth, the ground shook and trees fell. True to Tecumseh's words, the chief's village was destroyed.

Even in this age of science, we should be wary of thinking we know everything. The world is still a very mysterious place. Science has not answered all of the questions, even some of the most basic ones.

Scientists now believe, for example, that more than 90% of the universe is made of some unknown substance that we have never seen. They call it "dark matter." Everything in the world and all of the stars in the sky are, science tells us, just a small part of all that is really there.

Is this mysterious substance the Philosopher's Stone? Could dark matter be the world behind this one where Crazy Horse rode without being seen?

What is magic? What is not?

Do you believe in magic?

# Glossary

**Alchemy:** The magic of turning lead into gold.

**Charm:** A magical object carried for good luck. Also, a "hex" or "spell."

**Contortionist:** A person able to bend their body into unusual shapes.

**Elf:** A fairy who lives in a forest.

**Escape Artist:** An illusionist who specializes in escaping from things.

**Excalibur:** The magical sword King Arthur pulled from a stone.

**Fairy:** A nature spirit. Elves, gnomes, and leprechauns are different sorts of fairies.

**Fakir:** An illusionist of India who specializes in rope tricks.

**Holy Grail:** The magical cup thought to be the source of all things.

**Illusion:** Something that is not real. Tricks that imitate true magic.

**Leprechaun:** An Irish fairy often found under mushrooms.

**Magi:** Wise men and teachers of the ancient world. Magi believed all of nature was alive with unseen spirits and forces.

**Magic:** The science of the Magi. Power over unseen and perhaps supernatural forces.

**Philosopher's Stone:** A magical substance with the power to turn lead into gold.

**Science:** The study of nature. Magic that we can explain.

**Sorcerer:** A true magician.

**Supernatural:** More than natural. Something unusual or unexplained.

**Vision:** A magical dream that reveals secrets of nature.

**Witch:** A female magician thought to use "dark powers."

**Wizard:** A true magician.